AMERICAN BARNS

IN A CLASS BY THEMSELVES

by Stanley Schuler

Dear Sandy
Merry Christmas 1990
Reg. Mike

Schiffer Publishing Ltd

1469 Morstein Road, West Chester, Pennsylvania 19380

Printed in the United States of America.
ISBN: 0-88740-145-7
Published by Schiffer Publishing Ltd.
1469 Morstein Road, West Chester, Pennsylvania 19380

This book may be purchased from the publisher.
Please include $2.00 postage.
Try your bookstore first.

TABLE OF CONTENTS

How farmyards grow. An old Pennsylvania bank barn surrounded by modern barns and related buildings.

IN A CLASS BY THEMSELVES

In any listing of the world's many different types of building—houses, churches, office buildings, factories and so on—you cannot easily rank the importance of barns. But barns most certainly stand near the top because we could not get along without them. They protect our food after harvest and also before (livestock and poultry). They protect the seeds and feed from which food comes. They protect the farm implements and machinery that facilitate growth of food. In early days they protected our means of locomotion—horses, mules, oxen, carts, carriages—and still do to some extent. Yet encyclopedias make almost no mention of barns.

In architecture, barns have no standing whatever. Only a handful have been designed by architects. Until prefabricated barns entered the picture, all were homemade. Whoever designed them, all are plain, unassuming buildings.

And although barns total several millions, they number well below houses and many kinds of commercial structure.

Yet barns are among our most beloved buildings. Why?

You can readily understand why farmers and other barn owners (of whom there are thousands; the number is growing steadily) feel strongly about barns. To them they are a utilitarian necessity. But why is it that, when I mention that I am writing a book about barns, at least one person—usually more—in the surrounding circle invariably exclaims, "You are really? I love barns. Have you seen—?"

Admittedly, there are just as many people in the same circle that are left cold by barns. They think my book is an amusing, somewhat asinine diversion. But such considerable lack of interest cannot alter the fact that millions of non-farming city dwellers and suburbanites feel a warm sympathy for barns.

Are they simply nostalgic? If as children they ever lay in a hay loft, sucking on a straw and dreamily breathing in the sweet aroma of the dry grass, they may be. But if they have never had any real contact with barns, I don't see how they can be nostalgic about them.

Are they being appreciative of the importance of barns to life now and in the past? Never.

Do they see something romantic about an ancient barn that gradually comes to make them feel that all old barns are romantic? In some instances, this is more than likely. In Michigan I was telling a young urban couple about my search for barns and they immediately said, "You must see the one just south of Flint on I-10. It's gorgeous. We love it. We're crazy about barns but this is our favorite." So I went to see it—and passed it by. I could not fathom what there was about the old sway-backed derelict that made them ecstatic. Yet in them it had sparked a great enthusiasm for barns in general.

Do people feel a personal connection with barns even though they do not actually have one? All of us feel a personal connection with houses. Except for agnostics, we feel a comparable connection with churches. We have no such feeling for factories, office buildings, stores and the like. Barns fall somewhere between these extremes. Whether we're conscious of it or not, we feel a link with barns because we know they have a direct bearing on our well-being. But this alone is not enough to instill a love for barns.

Or do people really see beauty in barns and admire and cherish them in the same way that they react to a beautiful home, a painting or tree? This I suspect comes closest to the mark.

Because there is beauty in barns. It's the same beauty you see in early colonial homes. Barns have simplicity. Integrity. Strength. Warmth.

They have color and texture—often great texture.

And they are very frequently sited in pretty ranging to magnificent settings.

True enough, not all barns have beauty. In fact, the majority do not if you discount the effect that the surrounding countryside has on them. They are utility buildings—no more, no less.

True enough, among beautiful barns some are more beautiful than others. I deplore the parochialism of Pennsylvanians for Pennsylvania barns and New Englanders for New England barns. But I must admit that, on average, these two groups of barns are outstanding. On the other hand, there are equally beautiful individual barns in every corner of the United States. They just aren't so numerous.

American barns are in a class by themselves. Of course Europe has excellent barns, too. But from the time that our first settlers were reasonably certain they were going to survive in the New World and began to put down permanent roots, barns assumed unusual importance here; and this importance has grown as we became the bread basket of the world.

Three hundred years ago European barns and houses were commonly a single structure, with people and animals living more or less together. But the early American's first home was a hovel; his livestock was left outdoors. Later, when he got around to barn-building, he not only placed the barn at some distance from his house but also built it to sizable proportions.

The separation of barn from house was partially attributable to the fact that the earliest settlers lived together in stockaded communities for protection against Indians, and there was no room for barns. Separation was also dictated by the fact that in our colder climates the need for weathertight barns to protect food supplies was more important than the need for comfortable dwellings, and they therefore were built first.

The large size of American barns stemmed in part from their separation (why build small when there was ample space to do otherwise?). But the climate was mainly responsible. In the long, cold, wet winters of New England and New York, Pennsylvania and New Jersey, big barns were necessary to shelter the livestock and its feed as well as some of the families' foodstuffs.

Actually, these explanations of why American barns were built as large, separate structures from early times are somewhat conjectural. But it is undeniable that Americans (and Canadians) started building barns in a big and different way long, long ago, and they continued to do so down to the present. The recreation of early Plymouth called Plimouth Plantation does not have barns because researchers have been unable to determine that barns existed in Plymouth before 1627, the cut-off date for the Plantation. But there are references to barns in 1639 deeds, and a 1640 contract for construction of a barn in Rumney Marsh, north of Boston, called for a structure "72 foot in length & 26 foot wide & 10 foot high (at the side walls) with 2 porches each of 13 foot wide one way &

12 another". This was somewhat larger than the average barn built in eastern England in the 17th Century.

The word "barn" automatically brings to the American mind a large, rectangular, two-story structure surmounted by a steep gable roof. It is made of wood; has few if any windows and a huge double door. It is usually painted dark red (the color long ago chosen because red paint was durable, easily made and contributed to barn warmth by absorbing the rays of the sun).

On a smaller scale and without the red paint, this was probably the barn of the 1700s and late 1600s. "Probably", I say, because our forebears left little in writing to explain their barn-building and because few if any of the earliest barns have survived the onslaught of natural aging, windstorms, lightning, fire and, today, real estate developers.

But as you travel the country and take a close look at our barns, you cannot fail to notice that they are not so stereotyped as generally thought. True, most come from the same mold but it is a very flexible mold.

The early barn was a multi-purpose structure. It housed cows, oxen, horses, hogs, sheep, poultry on the ground floor. In the cavernous space above was a mountain of hay. Tucked in here and there were farm implements, feed grains, seeds and what not. In the center of the barn, at the level that wagons were drawn in for unloading hay, was the threshing floor, but in other than harvest season, it too, was used for miscellaneous storage.

To house these many things and activities, the barn was framed with great timbers, usually of oak, pegged together. The timbers were assembled in a series of Hs. The principal H frames were transverse—perpendicular to the roof ridge—and, depending on the length of the barn, there were three or four or more of them. The uprights rose from floor to roof. The crosspieces were set high above the floor so loaded wagons could pass below.

The H frames were tied together by timbers running the length of the barn, from gable end to gable end. Across the tops of the posts were the purlin-plates that were the main support of the roof. Below these, about at the height of the eaves, was another longitudinal row of timbers. And sometimes there was a third row below these, roughly ten feet above the floor.

The side walls of the barn were set well out from the H frames. They were framed with large, widely spaced posts set between the sill-plate and top-plate. Transverse beams placed at eaves height connected them to the H frames.

Viewed from front or back, the barn was divided into three wide aisles, called bays. Similarly, seen from the sides, the barn was divided into transverse bays, the number depending on the number of H frames.

Basic barn framing. Drawing is greatly simplified. Big H frames topped by purlin-plates are main supports of barn.

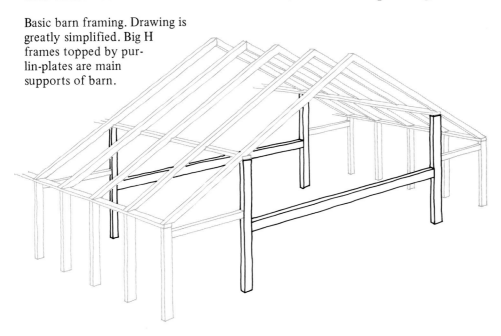

KMA Graphics

Above the main floor, the barn had several levels. These were not solidly floored. Instead, planks or, in the old days, poles were thrown across the transverse beams. They were all the farmer needed for storage of hay in the upper part of the barn, and the open spaces between planks assured circulation of air up through the mow.

The barn roof was composed of large, long, well spaced rafters that were joined at the ridge (either to a ridge board or to one another), supported more or less at midpoint by the purlin-plates, and tied to the top-plates at the eaves. The sheathing planks were laid across the rafters and the shingles were nailed to these.

The barn walls were made of boards installed either horizontally or vertically. The wagon door was generally centered in the front wall. Frequently there was a similar doorway in the back wall or sometimes one of the side walls so that a wagon could be drawn right through the barn instead of being backed out after loading or unloading.

The other principal opening into the barn was the hay-loft door placed close under the peak of the roof, usually at the front of the barn.

Windows were few, far between and often erratically placed. Natural lighting was not and still is not considered necessary. Neither were windows used much for ventilation.

But good ventilation was vital. This apparently was not widely recognized in very early times. Then air was admitted to barns mainly through small holes of various shapes in the gable ends. But as farmers came to realize that barn fires were often caused by not-quite-dry hay bursting spontaneously into flame, the size, number and design of air-intake holes in the walls increased greatly. Further to improve passage of air, the farmers added cupolas. But barns without cupolas or modern metal roof ventilators exceed the number with.

This you might call our "basic barn". But if all American barns were like it, looking at them would not be much fun.

However, it is fun because barns vary so widely.

Framing methods have changed. This has not altered the exterior appearance of barns very much. But inside, new barns — especially those used primarily for the garaging of huge, complex farm machines — are unlike old because the H frames have disappeared. Roofs are now supported on trusses bearing on the side walls (as in many modern houses and factories). The result is that barn interiors are free of posts that divide the large space into small spaces and that impede the movement of tractors, trucks, combines, etc.

The multi-purpose barn is giving way to the specialized barn. Of course the multi-purpose barn is still very much with us. For one thing, many farmers still raise more than one kind of crop or raise one crop, such as corn, for the production of another crop, such as hogs. Then, too, many one-crop farmers — dairymen, apple-growers and so on — are still using the multi-purpose barns they inherited from their fathers and grandfathers. After all, farmers are essentially thrifty folk and they don't lightly discard a sound barn just because they've switched crops. They adapt it to their new requirements instead.

But farming in this century is becoming increasingly specialized, one farmer producing just wheat, another just peaches, another just milk. Accordingly, as old barns collapse or burn or become too expensive to maintain or too inconvenient to use, their owners build a new barn designed to their specific needs. In most cases, this is a metal prefab that, from an aesthetic standpoint, has no appeal at all. Our old barns may not be architectural masterpieces, but they tower high above prefabs not only in actuality (prefabs are essentially one-story structures) but also in appearance.

Be that as it may, the specialized barn does add interest to barn-looking. Just as silos, which date back to 1873, added a new dimension to the farmyard so have the shiny low prefabs. To the confirmed urbanite or suburbanite who berates the farmers for the food prices he pays and who thinks of farming as an archaic industry, the new buildings are evidence that farming is a very progressive science. Most of all, perhaps, the new barns accentuate the beauty of the old.

Even the multi-purpose barn has been surrounded by specialized buildings. This very probably began happening a couple of centuries ago. Even though the farmer who raised several different crops was perfectly content with his multi-purpose barn, he found that he needed additional more specialized buildings—a henhouse, corn crib, toolhouse, hog shed, smokehouse, cattle-feeding shelter and so on. So while some farms still have only one barn, many others have a whole collection of buildings grouped around the big barn.

It may be stretching a point to call these ancillary structures barns but I include several of them in this book because they are an integral part of our farms, are used like barns for storage and animal housing, and are often interesting structures in their own right.

Two kinds of barn have always played specialty roles. Horse barns, or stables are one. Carriage houses—the precursors of the modern garage and often used as a garage—are the other.

Unlike the "basic barn", stables are generally one-story buildings, long and narrow. They have lots of windows and often have a door into each stall. And perhaps because racing is the sport of kings, thoroughbred stables are likely to be designed to suit a king. More plebeian horses such as Morgans and stock horses have much simpler quarters.

Carriage houses, on the other hand, are almost always modestly dressy structures in keeping with the houses to which they are related. Only big homes owned by rich people had carriage houses for the safekeeping of vehicles, horses and the horses' fodder. The country doctor, average attorney or druggist kept his horse and buggy in a much more modest building that he called a barn.

Barns vary with the region and the people that built them. Best known are the Pennsylvania Dutch and New England barns.

The former is also known as the bank barn, and more properly so because it is not restricted to the areas in Pennsylvania that were settled by the Germans and Swiss. The same barns are found in other German settlements, where they are sometimes called basement barns.

The bank barn had two completely separate levels and wherever possible was built on a south-facing slope. The lower floor was dug out of the hillside and so corresponded to the half-below-ground-half-above-ground basement of a hillside house. The livestock was kept here and let in and out of a walled or fenced cattlepen through a series of heavy Dutch doors. Since this floor opened only to the south and was shielded from north winds by the hill, it gave the animals excellent protection against bitter cold.

The ceiling of the lower level, which was roughly eight to ten feet high, was made of thick planks laid across massive post-supported beams and heavy joists. It formed the floor of the upper level, which had a great door opening directly to the hillside so the farmer could drive his wagons straight in. This part of the barn, which was roughly 25 feet high, was constructed like the "basic barn"; and here the farmer stored his hay, grain, meals and rolling stock and did his threshing.

In most Pennsylvania bank barns the main (upper) part of the structure overhung the lower part on the south side by as much as ten feet. This was called the forebay or overshoot. Other bank barns were built without it but acquired it later when the south wall of the upper section was pushed out to expand storage space.

One other important feature of bank barns built in Pennsylvania is their extensive stonework. The Germans that settled the United States evidently were better masons and believed more in masonry construction than the English and other nationalities because in a high percentage of Pennsylvania Dutch barns the end walls were stone from the ground all the way to the roof peak, and in some barns the north wall was also stone. These magnificent thick (eighteen to thirty-inch) walls do far more to distinguish the barns than the hex signs usually associated with them.

New England barns, on the whole, have no such stand-out characteristics. True, more of them have cupolas than barns in other regions; and the cupolas are more varied and lovelier. And when the roof peak is extended out over the hay-loft door to form a rain-hood, it is usually pointed like the bow of a ship whereas hoods elsewhere are larger and blunted. But if you were to move a group of New England barns to the Middle West, you probably could not pick them out of the crowd. They are simply plain wood-sided "basic barns"; and if, en masse, they appear weather-beaten and craggy—like the stereotyped Maine Yankee—you are just being unduly influenced by the natural backdrop against which they are set.

What people think of as the New England barn—a definite style of barn—is actually found almost exclusively in Maine, New Hampshire and Vermont, and while common enough there, it still is in the minority. This is the barn that is attached to the house by a string of small subsidiary buildings such as a woodshed, toolhouse and milkhouse. "Continuous architecture" is a term occasionally used to describe the elongated structure, which runs in straight lines, turns corners and even darts off at an angle. Were you to pull it apart, you would have a conventional house at one end, a conventional barn at the other end, and an assortment of conventional little buildings between. What, then, is the reason for it? To permit the farmer and his family to walk from house to barn or intermediate buildings without venturing into deep snow and sub-zero temperatures.

I once asked a Wisconsin farmer why his state, Minnesota, northern Michigan and the Dakotas don't have New England barns. "Dunno," he said. "Our winters sure are bad enough." He paused, then added: "I don't need one anyway. We go to Florida come winter." Which is hardly the answer today and certainly wasn't before Florida became our principal winter vacationland.

In addition to New England and Pennsylvania Dutch barns there are other region-related or builder-related categories of barn, but they are not so well known.

The Dutch barn is a distinct type built by early immigrants from Holland who settled in New York state, primarily along the Hudson and Mohawk Rivers and Schoharie Creek. There are no longer many of them. Professor John Fitchen in his book, *The New World Dutch Barn*, lists only seventy-six, although he says there are more, including a few in New Jersey.

At first glance the Dutch barn looks much like the "basic barn" and it is framed in the same way. However, it formed a rectangle a little wider than long and was topped by a gable roof that sloped toward the sides (whereas in most buildings, the gable roof has a ridge paralleling the long walls and the roof slopes toward these). It was built all of wood with either horizontal board siding or, sometimes, shingles. It had only one floor, which farm wagons originally entered from either gable end. Cantilevered out over both doors were shallow shed roofs called pentices.

Inside, the barn had three front-to-rear aisles, the center one about twice as wide as either of the side aisles. The framing was massive. This was particularly true of the beams that formed the crosspieces of the H frames. They measured as much as twelve by twenty-four inches. But most unusual was the fact that the tenons joining them with the mortises in the uprights extended through the uprights and a foot or so beyond. The protruding ends were often neatly rounded off.

The crib barn is the barn most typical of the South and Southwest. Actually, it is far from being the predominant barn because the area has all kinds of barns, including "basic barns" and countless open sheds with gently sloping roofs that extend well beyond the supporting posts.

The crib barn is a lovely, gentle-looking barn. It is not so tall as northern barns but it is very wide and usually quite shallow. It looks as if it were built in three sections: a tall one in the middle with identical low wings on either side. A single gable roof, however, covers the entire structure. This bends slightly upward like a bent arm where the side sections join the middle.

In the earliest crib barns the middle section was built of horizontal logs placed close together, and in the wings the logs or planks were spaced as in a corn crib. Today, boards or metal sheets are used. They are often installed vertically without air spaces between; and in some cases, they are entirely omitted from one or more of the walls in the side sections.

The transverse crib barn is a larger version of the standard crib barn. It was made, in effect, by placing two crib barns face to face but several feet apart, thus creating a transverse wagon-way through the barn in addition to the wagon-way running from front to back. The barn also had shed-roofed wings on front and back and connected to the side wings. One huge roof covered the entire structure.

Remodeling has changed the appearance of countless barns. Instead of putting up new buildings, farmers often gain the new space or facilities they require by remodeling and enlarging their main barns. This rarely enhances the beauty of the barns, especially when the addition is a shed-roofed structure tacked on to the sides or end of a big two or three-story barn.

The addition of a long, narrow gable-roofed wing looks better.

But from an architectural standpoint, remodeling is most successful when a wing of the same proportions and design as the barn is added. This results in enormous L-shaped, T-shaped, U-shaped or cross-shaped structures that dominate everything around them.

And then there are round barns and polygons. Not many, to be sure. But when you chance upon one in some totally unexpected part of the country, it is cause for excitement. These are handsome structures and almost always imposing.

Round barns are rarely perfectly round. If made of wood, they generally have short flat sides in great numbers. Whether the perfect rounds were built before the "look-like" rounds—or vice versa—we don't know. But round barns are believed to have originated somewhere around 1825—perhaps a quarter of a century before octagonal barns, which came along with the octagonal houses popularized by Orson Squire Fowler.

Whatever the true history of these unusual barns, all were designed on the theory that there is more floor space and less wall space in a circle or polygon than in a rectangle. In most barns the silo was placed in the exact center and loaded, as silos are, at the top. The silage was forked out at the bottom and fed directly to the encircling cows, housed on the lowest level.

But for one reason or another, the barns did not work out so well as expected, and as far as I know, no big ones have been built since the early 1930s. A few small ones, however, have been put up by non-farmers with a few horses or sheep.

And stone barns. I don't include the Pennsylvania Dutch barns here even though they may be half or three-quarters stone. Some barns are entirely or almost entirely stone and they are generally ancient. English settlers built a few in the Philadelphia environs but most of those in eastern Pennsylvania and all in Texas and Missouri were German. Although of conventional barn design, all are gorgeous. Some credit for this goes to the arched doorways but mainly it goes to the beautiful texture of the stone.

Brick and concrete barns can be counted almost on your fingers.

And barns that fall into no category at all. A new residential development in Parker, Texas, just north of Dallas, has an amazing collection of these. Each of the substantial homes sits on a fenced acre (or more); each has a horse or two; and naturally each has a stable. These are not opulent-looking stables. They're just small, neat, attractive barns. All are akin to the hundreds of similar barns that are springing up in small towns and suburbs throughout the country, but each is a little different.

The Parker barns are representative of the present and future. But the past also had barns that cannot be categorized. They just didn't happen to be concentrated in one area. Examples are the Spanish-influenced horse barn on the King Ranch in Texas; the ring-shaped, turreted Timkin barn in Canton, Ohio; the druggist's charming little Greek Revival barn in Nauvoo, Illinois; the jewel of a carpenter Gothic barn in Chagrin Falls, Ohio; the enormous Victorian carriage house in Johnsonville, Connecticut.

Barn roofs take many shapes. In the beginning was the gable roof and the broken-gable roof of the crib barn. These are still the most common roof shapes. But the gambrel roof soon came into vogue because it increased hay-loft capacity, and you now see it everywhere.

Shed roofs are uncommon except on additions and on modified crib barns in which the side sections of the barn extend only part way up the walls of the middle section.

True saltbox roofs (known also as cat-slide roofs) are rare; and only occasionally is a shed roof attached to one slope of a gable roof to give the illusion of a saltbox. Eric Sloane has written that big barns of the Plains States often had saltbox roofs. The bottom edge of the long roof slope, which faced the prevailing wind, reached to within a couple of feet of the ground; and as winter came on, hay, cornstalks and sod were piled against the wall under this to keep cold out of the barn. But such barns seem to have disappeared.

Equilateral-arched, or rainbow, roofs are generally of more recent vintage. Barrel roofs date back only to the Quonset huts of World War II. (Some barrel-roofed barns are, in fact, Quonset huts set directly on the ground.) But neither of these is common.

If a census of barns was taken today, it would probably show that, nationwide, most roofs are clad with steel sheets. Asphalt-shingle roofs would be in second place. This, of course, is a comparatively recent development. Our first barns were either thatched or shingled with large chunks of bark. Since both materials had obvious disadvantages, they were soon replaced by wood shingles. Then came slate, which was fireproof and virtually indestructible. Many old barns still have their original slate roofs. In a few cases, the slates are laid out in attractive geometric patterns of several colors. In other cases, the date of barn raising is printed out in large numerals of a color contrasting with the color of the rest of the roof.

Decorative treatments are imaginative. They are also pretty rare. When he's feeling flush, the average American farmer keeps his barn painted. But he's never had much truck with architectural ornament or gingerbread (such fanciness is for the owners of carriage houses) or painted decorations.

There are, of course, exceptions. Here and there are farmers who have painted archways on their barn doors. A Michigan farmer celebrated the bicentennial by covering his entire barn and silo with the American flag and other appropriate red, white and blue decorations. Another Michigan farmer—or perhaps it was a pair of farmers—covered the end wall of one barn with a portrait of Beethoven and the corresponding wall of a second nearby barn with a portrait of Rembrandt.

But the most notable believers in painted decorations for barns are the Pennsylvania Dutch. In his book, *The Pennsylvania Dutch,** Fredric Klees, a Pennsylvania Dutchman himself, says: "...the decorations that brighten so many barns in Berks and Lehigh and other near-by counties...have often been mistaken for 'hex signs' to ward off evil; on the contrary, their purpose is a decorative one and for a long time has been only that. In the words of an Oley Valley farmer, they are 'for fancy'. A barn without them looks too plain, too naked. Pennsylvania Dutch farmers are proud of their barns and show their pride by adorning them with decorations. Centuries ago, long before these symbols were painted on Pennsylvania barns, they may have had some religious significance. August Mahr traces the star or lily pattern back to Crete, where it symbolized the sun as early as 1300 B.C.,

* Copyright 1950, and renewed 1983, by Fredric Klees.

and to Mycenae, where it existed about 1550 B.C. Much later it was regarded as a symbol of fertility in horses and cattle and was carved on barn doors or used on harness ornaments in central Europe. The six-petaled flower that appears so frequently in barn signs Mahr takes as a pre-Christian symbol of immortality; while the spinning whorl, quite a usual decoration on Lehigh County barns, was used not only in Crete but in ancient Troy. At one time the sort of symbols later painted on barns may have been intended to ensure fertility in the stock, to guard against lightning, and to keep out witches; but I have never come across a farmer who believes that barn symbols are anything but decoration. He thinks they look nice, and that is all. Whatever they may have been centuries ago, today they are only one more instance of the Pennsylvania Dutchman's love of the gaudy. Oddly enough, these signs were never painted on barns in Europe; that use was a Pennsylvania inspiration. Very similar decorations, however, appear on houses in the canton of Bern in Switzerland."

Other differences in barns are apparent to anyone who looks. Consider cupolas and roof ventilators. Wall ventilators. Rainhoods. Gable and dormer windows. Latches and other hardware. My pictures describe these better than words.

Just why these differences occur and the manner in which they occur are interesting matters, too.

Variations in the functional features of barns come about either because someone gets an idea, proves it works and other barn owners copy or because of basic changes in farming methods. For example, hay-loft doors are gradually disappearing because more and more farmers are using mechanical elevators to load in hay.

Variations in decorative features are equally explainable. If a farmer feels moved to decorate his barn, he either does it in his own way or imitates what someone else has done.

But why do all differences in barns tend to be so localized? Here are three cases in point:

Farmers in southern Wisconsin have a strong liking for rich-blue barn roofs. When you cross the state line into Iowa or Illinois, however, blue roofs almost instantly disappear.

The early German farmers in Amana, Iowa, thought it a good idea to build a deep canopy over the doors on the lower level of their barns. But farmers elsewhere have not followed suit.

Finally, in the small, rich valleys around Sunbury, Pennsylvania, almost all the Pennsylvania Dutch barns are ventilated by large louvered wall openings painted to stand out against the surrounding walls. Some of the openings are simple window-size rectangles; others are tall and narrow and arched like cathedral windows. They are stunning. More than that, they are effective and practical (except when they have to be painted). Yet you rarely see ventilators like them in other Pennsylvania Dutch barns.

Some localization of barn features can, no doubt, be attributed to the crops being grown. Some can be attributed to copy-catism. And in those rare instances when you see a feature here and then find it repeated within a restricted area five hundred miles to the west or south, localization can be attributed to the early-day migration of farmers from region to region.

The explanations don't really matter.

The important point is that there *are* so many variations in barns. To those who ignore or scoff at barns, these countless variations should prove that barns are not the humdrum buildings they think. To barn enthusiasts, they are evidence that barns are indeed very, very fascinating.

When the American forces were freezing and starving at
Valley Forge, this barn was standing. It is just on the
edge of the present park. General Henry Knox, quartered
in the nearby house, undoubtedly kept his horse here.

BANK BARNS

Above: This barn is typical of those built by the Pennsylvania Dutch though larger than many. The white-outlined doors in the forebay were used to toss hay down to the cattle in the big walled cattlepen on the south side of the barn. They also, of course, were used to fill the barn.

Opposite: A bank barn in Connecticut. The position of the door in the gable wall at right angles to the forebay is somewhat unusual. The door is customarily opposite the forebay but not always. Placement depended on how the barn was sited.

Favorite Pennsylvania Dutch signs are the star, sun, sunburst, lily or tulip, spinning whorl and inverted teardrop, but there are hundreds of variations, such as the four, six and eight-pointed star. Here are circled stars within larger circled stars. Two-part Dutch doors were almost invariably used under the overhanging forebay.

This Connecticut bank barn has been expanded into a U shape. The hay-loft door is unusual in that it slides up and down instead of being hinged at bottom. It is counter-weighted like a double-hung window.

This 1857 Ohio barn is beautifully landscaped, probably because it's in a residential area on a busy highway. A shed roof shelters the ground-level doors.

This Maine barn is built into a slope. Even so, soil has been hilled up high against it on the lower sides to increase protection against cold. Doorway in lower level is sheltered by a sort of vestibule. Door on opposite side leads into the upper level at eaves height.

German farmers were so partial to bank barns that they built them even on level land. As this Germantown, Wisconsin, barn indicates, livestock was quartered at ground level, protected by thick stone foundation walls. To reach the upper level, a big earthen ramp was built.

All these barns are in Connecticut. From the road, the barn on this page (right) looks like a small rainbow-roofed structure with some sort of wall beside it. From the back, it turns out to be a substantial structure with a shed-roofed addition. The little barn (opposite, top) is painted red and is a favorite of artists—not because it is in any way unusual but because of its lonely position in typical New England countryside. Opposite, bottom: Another small barn in the middle of a small town. The under-the-hill level is reached not only by the door on the side but also by one in back. You can get a better look at the exceptionally lovely trim on Page 224.

A matching pair of Pennsylvania barns set in an L to share one cattlepen, The slits in the wall of the facing barn were for ventilation. Early farmers did not ventilate barns as well as they do today.

This enormous barn in Pennsylvania is the equivalent of
a four-and-a-half-story house. Built in 1853, it replaced
a smaller barn. The wings were added later. The small
building in the corner of the cattlepen was a bull barn.

Details of the barn on Page 25 are shown at left and on the facing page. Like other Pennsylvania Dutchmen, the owner built to last, as evidenced by the stone gable walls. Not all farmers, however, ornamented their stone walls so handsomely. From the uphill side, the barn is entered, not on the second but the third level, via a buttressed ramp leading to a covered bridge. Below is the tiny barn used by a Pennsylvania motel to store mowers and other equipment on two levels. Built just a few years ago, it has grooved plywood siding.

Both barns are in Pennsylvania. The red one has stone end walls,

the yellow one does not. The cupolas on the former are especially attractive.

This is the front of the red barn shown on Page 28. The overall width of the bank of doors is very unusual. Three of the big doors, which slide, have hinged doors for people to use.

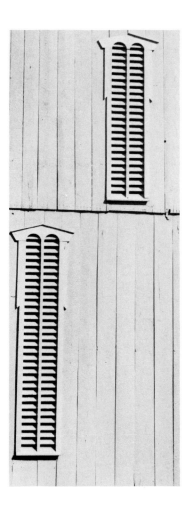

At left is a closeup of the louvered ventilators in the yellow barn on Page 29. The louvers are fixed, so the only way to shut off the flow of air through them is to cover the openings on the inside—and this is not done. Note the elegant proportions of the ventilators, the nice decorative details. Below is the framing in the original big barn. The area in the background was added.

The forebays on Pennsylvania Dutch barns are generally supported by the end walls. But in a few cases—usually when the forebay has been added—they are cantilevered. Here the forebay is supported by the stone wall at the left end and is cantilevered at the right end. Only one post was needed to provide additional support. (Posts under forebays are rather uncommon.)

Unless there was some compelling reason against it, Pennsylvania Dutch barns were always oriented to the south so that the lower level, where the livestock was kept, would be warmed by the low-hanging winter sun and snow would melt rapidly from the cattlepen.

The forebay of the Pennsylvania barn at left was added to the back of the original structure. This, however, is apparent only when you can look at the roof line. The Pennsylvania barn below is unusually small: the average barn measures about 40 by 60 feet. The wall set back under the forebay was removed so that the lower level could be used as a carport.

This barn, almost in downtown Allentown, has just about everything you would expect in a Pennsylvania Dutch barn: hex signs, fancifully painted doors, diamond-shaped wall ventilators. Just visible in the ivy at the left end (above) is a small "people" door with a rain-hood. Such hoods are characteristic of Pennsylvania Dutch barns.

Above: An almost entirely stone barn outside Philadelphia. The doorways on the lowest level are arched. They relieve the severity of the structure to some extent. Opposite are two old Amana, Iowa, barns. Amana barns are characterized by the deep shed-roofed hoods projecting over the livestock doors. The hoods' primary purpose was to shelter the farmer as he unloaded feed, loaded manure, etc.

L-shaped additions were made to these two already-big Pennsylvania bank barns.

Front (above) and back (right) of a rather severe Pennsylvania barn made lovely by its setting, cupola and gable window. Under the walled ramp up to the main door is a root cellar.

A Wisconsin bank barn with hex signs (which may have been imported from Pennsylvania since they're not painted directly on the barn). The chimney is extremely unusual: barns are not heated, mainly because of the danger of fire. This one may no longer be used for agricultural purposes.

The wood addition across the back of this ancient Pennsylvania stone barn has given it a slightly curved saltbox roof. The very short roof overhang at the gable is rather typical of Pennsylvania Dutch barns. The high walls of the ramp leading to the wood bridge guarantee against a wagon being driven off into the "moat".

This bank barn in Maine probably acquired the front wing after the original structure was built. Now it has an entrance to the upper level and to the lower level on the same side—a most unusual arrangement. The barn has a very New England look but it is not what is generally thought of as a New England barn.

CRIB BARNS

The beautiful barn on an equally beautiful farm at left is in Texas. That below is in Iowa. Both are modern modifications of the old crib barn. In the Texas barn the tall middle section is distinct from the wings on either side. The shed roofs of the wings do not reach quite to the top of the middle section's walls, thus leaving space for small clerestory windows. The Iowa barn is closer to the real crib barn, even having a slight break (bend) in each roof slope.

Barns like that at left are very common throughout our warmer regions and are seen in the North as well. This one is in northern Illinois. It is much like the larger Texas barn on Page 46 but without clerestory windows. Its relationship to the true crib barn below is evident.

There is no recognized name for the roof shape used on crib barns like that below (which is in Texas). It's called a reversed gambrel roof; also an interrupted gable roof. "Broken gable roof" seems best. It's far from perfect, especially for such an attractive roof.

Here are two old Georgia crib barns. That below is the standard crib barn (also called a double crib barn). On the opposite page is a transverse crib barn (the front of the barn at the top; the rear at the bottom). In this particular barn, the transverse wagon-way has been blocked off to

increase storage space. Yet another type of crib barn is the four-crib barn, which is much like the transverse barn in having sheds on four sides. It is, however, smaller. These pictures were taken by Yvonne Miller Brunton for her book, "Grady County, Georgia".

Preceding pages: A Texas barn—neglected,
little used, fast wearing out, but with great
appeal, which is primarily attributable to the
long graceful sweep of the roof.

Opposite, bottom: Hidden in a swale close below one of Louisiana's biggest and most beautiful Greek Revival plantation houses is this small crib barn, built in the very early 1800s. As the definite break in the roof indicates, the wings probably were added at a later date, though the vertical board siding is continuous. The bargeboards on the rakes are sawtoothed and the gable wall is peppered with holes for pigeons. Opposite, top: This Mississippi barn is quite different from the foregoing but is related in design. The big structure is built in three tiers. Below: The barn on a well-known Louisiana plantation is a cross between the other two and much more refined because it is directly behind the house. The bargeboards are scalloped; the doorway slightly peaked. There is a pigeon roost above the hay-loft door.

Ancient barn on famous Rosedown plantation at St. Francisville, Louisiana. Except for the siding, it is identical in front and back. The cribbed feed storage areas are protected from the heavy rains by the solid siding on the ends of the barn and by the shed overhangs. Note that the only foundations are brick piers.

The Tennessee barn (left) is like many in the western part of that state. It has the general contours of the crib barn; but the middle section is much taller and has a gambrel roof, while the side sections have very steep shed roofs. The rain-hood is typical of the area and is also widely used in the Middle West. Below: Kent Plantation house was built in 1796. The barn, which was part of the plantation, probably dates from about the same era. Both buildings have since been moved to Alexandria, Louisiana, are owned by the state and open to the public. The lower part of the middle section of the barn is made of squared logs. The neatly shaped entrances to the wings are probably a modern touch.

The argument can be made that these are not crib barns; nevertheless, they do belong to the crib-barn family. The modern Texas barns on this page do becasue of their conformation. The old Tennessee barns opposite do because of their crib-like bases. (After all, it is from their partially open construction that crib barns got their name.) Actually, according to John Rice Irwin, who took the pictures, the old barns are locally known as overhang or cantilever barns because the upper level projects twelve to fourteen feet out over the lower to provide shelter for livestock in extremely hot as well as wet weather. Mr. Irwin says that the extreme eastern part of Tennessee is one of the few U.S. regions in which this type of barn is found. He thinks it may be of German origin, which would account for the fact that the overhang is suggestive of Pennsylvania Dutch barns—particularly in the case of the barn at bottom. Both barns are now at the Museum of Appalachia in Norris, Tennessee.

NEW ENGLAND BARNS

Preceding pages: An unusually beautiful Maine barn connected by an unusually large wing to the house. The cupolas of the auxiliary buildings match that on the barn. Below: A New Hampshire barn.

Opposite: Two views of an extensive L-shaped barn complex in northern Maine. It was added to several times. The owner had an extraordinary liking for steep gables.

Jane Stanford

It takes heavier snow than this to keep a farmer in far-northern Maine indoors; but it is because of snow that he connects his house to his barn, thus creating the unique barn that is known as the New England barn. The barn below is also way up in Maine. The long wing at the right is a fairly recent addition. The canopy over the big door is unusual in New England but typical of old New York Dutch barns.

Jim Berry

The link between the Maine barn and house below is not so short as it appears here. It is now used as living quarters; it may have once served agricultural purposes.

New England barns are exceedingly rare—if not almost non-existent—in southern New England. That shown above and at the top of the facing page, however, is in Connecticut just a few miles from Long Island Sound. It was recently built by the owner of a firm, Country Designs, that sells plans for barns and related buildings of a New England flavor. The barn proper is smaller than the usual barn because it is used only as a workshop and, underneath, for boat storage. A variety of workrooms connect it to the house.

This is a lovely example of what is sometimes called "continuous architecture". Located in Maine, the barn is far removed from the little Cape Cod house, which was built in 1788. The barn is probably not so old.

The Ripking barn (above), south of Poughkeepsie, New York, is typical of Dutch barns except for the very slight bend in the lowest reaches of the roof. It is now abandoned. It measures 44 feet wide by 36 long. There are wagon doors in both gable ends. The pentice above the front door is characteristic of Dutch barns. The little white strips are pieces of aluminum someone recently added to protect the end joints between clapboards. The picture at right, taken in the barn on the next page, illustrates the New York Dutchman's framing methods. Note how the tenon of the massive crossbeam in the H frame extends far beyond the post. Timbers are oak and yellow pine.

DUTCH BARNS

To save it from destruction, the Verplanck-Van Wyck barn has been moved to Newburgh, New York, close to the old Dutch Colonial Verplanck house. The rectangular bay in the gable end is unique and unexplained, but it was probably built to shelter the door (in place of the customary pentice) and provide extra loft-storage space. The barn is roughly 50 feet wide and 44 feet long.

This is a faithful reconstruction of the little brick barn built by the druggist in the old Mormon settlement at Nauvoo, Illinois (the town from which Brigham Young led the Mormons to Utah). The stepped parapets at the gable ends are common to many Greek Revival structures. Despite its diminutive size, the barn is supported by posts and beams as much as 12 inches square.

ONE OF A KIND

The Timkin brick barn, in Canton, Ohio, is a ring with four turrets. It is now almost completely hidden by trees and shrubs; abandoned as a barn. But last year a fund-raising group advertised it as a haunted house and used it to extract money from children. The enormous barn on the opposite page is in Connecticut. It is no longer used as a barn either; a family calling it home rattles around in it like pebbles in a barrel. The multitudinous big windows give it much of its beauty, but pity the man who must paint them: each of those in front has fifty panes.

This big pink barn in Illinois has a roof that, if seen from above, is shaped like a four-pointed star. The cupola, painted green to match the upper reaches of the gable walls, has a similar roof. Opposite: Few barns can rival this one in Chagrin Falls, Ohio, in beauty. Its builder was imaginative and expert with tools. He saw to it that the barn was a fitting companion to the charming house behind the camera.

A few of the lovely details of the Victorian barn on the preceding page. Happily, the present owners are assiduous about keeping the building painted a glistening white. The colorful geometric figure in the ring under the roof peak is not glass but a glued-on painted decoration.

An odd Vermont barn. The main section, to which shed-roofed wings have been added, has a hip roof surmounted by a large, flat deck. The dormers are low and arched.

Gigantic U-shaped barn outside Philadelphia is just waiting for someone to save it from vandals and ultimate collapse. Opposite: Also near Philadelphia, this large stone structure is now a restaurant and clubhouse for a golf course. I thought at first it must have been extensively remodeled but was assured it had not been. This is the barn almost exactly as built (primarily for dairying) several decades ago by a wealthy man who must have imagined he lived in Europe. The tower is one of the silos. The cylindrical cupola conceals a metal ventilator.

MASONRY BARNS

The barn below and the even larger barn on the preceding pages are in Missouri. Except for the wood addition on the side of the barn here, they were built entirely of local stone. The doorways were arched (as was usually the case in old stone barns) so they could carry the weight of the walls above. The numerous slits in the walls of the preceding barn were for ventilation; but the builder of this one apparently did not worry about such things. The pictures were taken by Piaget for Charles van Ravenswaay's book, "German Houses in Missouri".

The Shakers were good farmers and built excellent large barns. These they liked to make of stone, although they also used wood. This was one of the barns in the Shaker Community at Harvard, Massachusetts. It is a bank barn. The interior picture is of the third level.

From the collections of the Library of Congress

Stone barns are fairly prevalent on the eastern edges
of the Texas hill country, where many Germans, direct
from the old country, settled in the 1840s and 50s. This
long saltbox is an example. The stonework was extensively repaired at some time by men not so expert as the original masons; and it is possible that the left end (above,
right) was added. The barn is ventilated through the
slatted gable ends.

This Texas barn is within stone's throw of that on the preceding pages. The barn evidently began life as a leanto, as evidenced by the rough stonework (below); then the main body was added. Despite the rude half doors, the arched entrances are handsome. These may seem too elaborate for such a simple building, but as noted earlier, a well-built arch could support the walls above it. Doorways with a flat head would have required a steel or heavy wood lintel. In central Texas, steel was probably too valuable to be used and trees yielding large straight timbers were scarce.

Below: A tiny Texas barn. The high, little windows—barely more than slits in the gable end and only about a foot square in front (behind the tree)—make one wonder if the barn was not also designed to serve as a fort during Indian raids.

The barns at left and below are built of adobe. Both are near Las Cruces, New Mexico. The former is a Territorial-style structure as indicated by the flat roof (possible because the area has less than eight inches of rainfall a year), the bare minimum number of door and window openings, and the once-decorative trim in the top four courses of brick. The barn is probably one hundred years old or more. The traditional barn below is younger. Note the two buttresses reinforcing the left wall. The wood lintel over the door carries the wall above.

When labor was plentiful and cheap, adobe barns were common in the Southwest. They are almost never built today because they cost more than wood or metal barns. But they served—and still serve—farmers in the region well. The twelve to eighteen-inch-thick walls are excellent insulation against heat and extremely sturdy (rapid deterioration occurs only when they begin to crack or lean). Since there is so little rain, the large straw-reinforced mud bricks are not eroded by moisture. The wear that is visible in the pictures is the result of years and years of sandblasting by violent spring windstorms.

Robert Coughlin

Above: Another Texas barn, this one interesting because of the high curving stone wall that partially enclosed a cattlepen. The roof overhang on all these Texas barns is, for most part, minimal since rainfall is low in central Texas; therefore, there is no great need to shed roof water far to the sides of the buildings. Opposite: On the Johns Hopkins University campus in Baltimore, this handsome, ivy-covered brick structure is known simply as The Barn, though it now serves as a center for extracurricular activities. But it was a dairy barn, financed in 1800 by Charles Carroll, a signer of the Declaration of Independence, as a wedding present for his son. Young Carroll's extravagance in building and refining the barn (and house that went with it) was such that his father often complained. And when the young man announced his intentions to knock out portions of the dairy wall and put in two windows, his father wrote: "I can compare your building to nothing better than Penelope's web. You have done and undone, and by that way greatly added to the expenditures." Whether the barn worked out well functionally we do not know, but there is no questioning its beauty. Once completed, it was not much changed. The wings, however, were added, but not by the Carrolls and not for any agricultural purposes.

The massive poured-concrete barn and smaller barn on this page were built in Pennsylvania after fire destroyed an earlier barn and the owner swore it would never happen again. The barn is not otherwise unusual except in the way it was constructed. The floors of the second and third stories are concrete. The gambrel roof is supported by an unusual system of 2 x 10s bolted together as shown. The lowest floor, for the dairy herd, was ventilated by huge concrete ducts (of which one is shown) that rose to the rooftop. Opposite is a Pennsylvania bank barn made of a greenish stone called serpentine. More pictures of this beautiful 1820 structure are on the next pages.

94

Three sides of the barn shown on the preceding page were built of serpentine; the front, with the bridge to the ramp, is of fieldstone. Note the keystone in the doorway arches; the keystoned arch over the gable window. The mason scratched his name and date in two places: no one can say he did not deserve to be remembered.

A local historian maintains that this slit-ventilated stone bank barn in Pennsylvania was constructed by an English farmer although the area was settled by the Pennsylvania Dutch many generations ago. Whatever its origin, it was sturdily and beautifully built.

The bridge to this stone bank barn near Philadelphia is highly unusual because it, too, is of stone and has an arched doorway like the doorway and large windows in the south wall. Even the springhouse at the right has an arched doorway.

ROUND AND POLYGONAL BARNS

Seen in the morning mist, a twenty-sided Vermont barn looks almost perfectly round. The silo in the center rises well above the roof peak.

This Iowa barn forms a perfect circle. It is built of structural clay tile. The man who put it up during the Great Depression is reputed to have gone broke in the process and to have lost the entire farm.

Miranda S. Burnett

Above is a sixteen-sided New Hampshire barn. Unlike most, the roof is stepped. The California barn opposite has so many sides that you lose count trying to add them all up. But it's called round because it looks it. Actually, the truly round barns are made of small building blocks —stones, bricks, tiles. To make a wood barn round would have required too much shaping of the siding boards unless they were installed vertically (as some were).

Hal Simkover

A ten-sided Iowa barn with the silo running down through
the center. The silo was filled through the flat chute on the
side of the above-roof extension. In most round barns, the
silo had a small window or door through which corn was
loaded. The silage was fed to the cows encircling the silo
at the base of the barn.

Above: An octagonal Pennsylvania barn. At right: A round barn in Wisconsin. The latter was built in 1911 as a dairy barn. It is now used for apple storage.

A pair of octagonal barns in Wisconsin. The red one is now at Old World Wisconsin, an outdoor museum at Eagle. It was dismantled and moved there several years ago from

Mequon. Approximately ninety years old, it was one of a
dozen or so octagonal barns built around Mequon by
Ernst Clausing.

This is the only octagonal barn built by Ernst Clausing that remains in Mequon, Wisconsin. Except for that on the preceding page, all have been torn down by developers or destroyed by fire or storm. As the picture above shows, the barn does not have an inside silo. The roof slants up from all sides to the peak, which is crowned by a small round cupola made of miniature columns under a hat-shaped top. As a result, the barn interior is a towering, cavernous, completely open space. To reach this vast room, the farmer drove his wagons up a ramp, which is more or less at the back of the building as seen in the color photo. Livestock was quartered at ground level where the picture at left was taken. The posts and beams supporting the upper level are roughly 12 x 12 inches in cross-section. The beams are about 33 feet long.

The most famous round barn is the Shaker stone barn at Hancock, Massachusetts. Built in 1826, it was burned out about forty years later; then rebuilt. It is 270 feet in circumference. The stone walls are up to three-and-a-half feet thick and twenty-one high. The almost flat-roofed structure above is a wood polygon surmounted by a towering octagonal cupola.

The barn differs from others in that the open-sided central shaft serves as a ventilating duct. Hay is stored around this from the main floor up. Up to fifty-two head of cattle were housed around this on the main floor. A ramp (opposite, top) took wagons to the second floor, where they could drive all the way around the barn above the cattle. When the barn was rebuilt, the space below the cattle was dug out to serve as a manure pit. It was high enough for wagons to circulate in.

The two long rectangular wings were added some time after the rebuilding.

From the collections of the Library of Congress

The octagonal barn opposite is in Connecticut. It was recently built on a large residential property to house a few riding horses and farm animals.

I do not mean to disparage the barns in this section of the book when I refer to them as "Just Barns". They are as fine as any others. They just don't happen to fall into any neat category. The Indiana barn above, for instance, is a plain, straight-forward structure with one unusual feature: Instead of protecting the hay-loft opening with a small rain-hood, the farmer let the entire roof overhang the gable wall about three feet. Note that the loft door hangs open. Because of its weight and since it is hinged at the bottom, it is no fun to close.

JUST BARNS

A huge L-shaped barn in Tennessee. The back wing was probably added. As a rule, additions to barns detract from the appearance of the structure. But when the addition more or less matches the original barn, as here, the result is usually attractive. The flare given to the gambrel roof is quite common in gambrel-roofed barns everywhere. It enhances the lines of the roof.

The charming small Massachusetts barn at right was designed by the Boston architectural firm of Royal Barry Wills Associates, which is famed for its New England colonial houses. (A few other modern barns are architect-built; but almost none of the old ones was.) The barn has much the look of a Cape Cod house. The woodshed wing is Modern but complements the barn nicely.

Above: A brand new Connecticut barn with garage wing. Built by a family that uses the property only as a weekend retreat, it is presently meant only for storage of gardening equipment; but it is large enough for the horses or livestock that may come later.

Above: Rainbow roofs are expensive to build but generally add charm and distinction to barns. They also increase storage space in the loft. This small barn-garage is in Massachusetts. The ground floor has stone walls. Left: Small barn on a Louisiana plantation. Because the livestock can be allowed to roam in all seasons in the deep South, barns generally are not large. But the sheds used for farm machinery are frequently huge.

Below: Multi-gabled barns are fairly common in New England. This one is owned by a Connecticut historical society and used as a small museum. Right: This barn, of about the same vintage, is in an Ohio town. The overhead garage door is an unfortunate change but understandable. If you use an old barn as a garage, you don't really want to contend with outswinging barn doors.

Opposite, top: The board-and-batten gable end of this Mississippi barn contrasts nicely with the brick walls. X-braced doors are always attractive. Bottom: This three-fourths-enclosed shed in Connecticut is used for storage of hay and farm machines.

Above: This old barn is connected with the Kammlah house, now the Pioneer Museum, in Fredericksburg, Texas. Just why it is two-thirds stone and one-third wood is a question, but the combination is attractive.

Contrasting designs in gambrel roofs. The barn below is in Arkansas. The hay-loft doors are exceptionally large. The barn at left is in Texas while the small one below it is in Louisiana. Note that the eaves roof on the left side of the latter has the same slope as the shed roof on the right. This is a very minor thing but shows careful attention to aesthetic detail.

The rainbow roof makes this a truly handsome barn (fresh white paint helps, too). The roof design is repeated in the small wing at left and big wing at right and also in the dormers and a smaller nearby barn.

Nagler

If this Connecticut barn were a house, it would be called a dogtrot house because an open corridor runs through it. You are looking at the back of the barn. Here the main floor is reached by a long ramp. There's a root cellar below the ramp and driveways to the red-doored garages on both sides. In front, the main floor of the barn is at ground level. In other words, this is a sort of reverse bank barn. The fenestration is unusual.

Above: A neat modern Maine barn with board-and-batten siding on the walls and clapboards on the gable ends.

A larger barn next door to that on the opposite page. It is used mainly as a workshop, which accounts for the long strip windows. As shown on the opposite page, these are simply but cleverly made of large sheets of glass laid against the studs and held in place by the exterior casings.

Opposite page: A barn in the old Mormon settlement at Nauvoo, Illinois. On this page is a fairly new barn-garage in Connecticut. It was built in an ancient stone-walled cattlepen to replace one blown down in a hurricane. It has a saltbox roof.

On this page are three modern barns. The flat-top above is a new kind of metal prefab. At right is a Quonset hut. Both are in Texas. Below is a Quonset-hut relative with a rainbow roof. It is in Ontario. On the facing page is an old Wisconsin barn that is being torn down. For anyone intent on saving the valuable lumber, demolition is about as difficult as putting up a new barn of the same type.

The dormers on the Texas barn at the top of the facing page were added. The long row of windows in the side of the red Vermont barn is unusual because most barns are nearly windowless. The New Jersey barn above stretches well to the left of the camera lens. The corn crib in the foreground is typical of those used in the East but larger than most. The sign indicates that the farm is or was to be turned into a development.

A few barns have dormers—generally shed dormers; and now that mechanical conveyors are used to load hay bales into lofts, the dormers sometimes serve as points of access to the loft. The big dormer on a rather nondescript Connecticut barn at right, however, was designed specifically as a loft door. Barns like the large, low Tennessee structure below are quite common in the South.

Automobiles have not helped the appearance of barns because the garages for them are often tacked onto the old buildings. But despite its typically unattractive doors, this garage has done less damage than most since the addition is in scale with the barn (in Ohio) and has a roofline to match. The cupola with its gnome-like hat is an original. There are many unusual and charming cupolas in this book—all worth close study.

Above: A northern Maine barn with shed dormers (see Page 138). The little Connecticut barn at right is extremely simple but made attractive by its setting and unusual color. The owners have even installed shutters to soften the otherwise bleak lines. As on a great many barns, the big X-braced door hangs from a track and slides across the wall. This installation method greatly eases opening and closing and prevents the sagging that occurs in large hinged doors. But the track and hangers are not items that can be purchased in the ordinary hardware store.

Opposite, top: A handsome Arkansas barn. Bottom: This
one is in Tennessee. Above: A pair of New York barns
with unusual cupolas. The owner took advantage of the
fact that he lived near Vermont's quarries and put slate
on the roofs. He was not, however, content with just ordinary roofs. Instead the barn and cupola roofs are decorated with stars and bands made of dark-colored slates.

The shed-roofed extension was built along with this new Connecticut barn to give adequate depth for farm machinery (the main body of the barn is only about fifteen feet deep). The owner chose this design because the two roofs could be framed with short rafters rather than the long ones normally used in the rear slope of a saltbox roof. But the owner is rather embarrassed about his failure to match the three doorways.

This Ohio barn was recently extensively remodeled to make space for combines and other large farm equipment. The front door was increased in height and width and the enormous shed-roofed section was added.

Framework of the barn on Page 144 (left) and of the original gambrel-roofed section of the barn on Page 145 (right). The latter was designed to eliminate interior posts and

increase headroom so there would be more free space for maneuvering machinery. It was also designed so the barn would sway in gales sweeping off nearby Lake Erie.

Above: Companion barns in New Hampshire. Opposite, bottom: A small Connecticut barn partially converted to a garage. Top: A modern Iowa barn with the open, hood-ed wagon-way favored by Amana farmers.

The gambrel roof of the fog-shrouded Ohio barn above is of conventional shape, but the pointed rain-hood over the loft door makes it look peculiar. The Maine barn at left may be exactly what the owner wants but it looks too tall for its width. The gambrel-roofed Connecticut barn opposite is better proportioned from an architectural standpoint. At top, opposite, is a small Connecticut cattle barn-shed.

Three barn complexes in Ohio. In the picture above, which does not show all the buildings, note that the square cupola is set at a 45-degree angle to the ridge.

Canadian barns are very similar to those in the U.S. But the New Brunswick barn (opposite, top) has what is known as a clipped or snub-nosed gable roof. Some barns in northern Maine have the same kind of roof. The Ontario barn below is different only in that the wagon door is at one end rather than in the middle of the front wall.

Carriage houses follow no pattern; are invariably much more highly styled than barns; and usually have at least some of the architectural characteristics of the house to which they're related. This one in Mississippi exemplifies the first two points but is quite unlike the famous antebellum mansion that it serves.

CARRIAGE HOUSES

The glorious carriage house on Pages 156 and 157 and opposite is in Johnsonville (part of East Haddam), Connecticut. It is occasionally open to the public, but you can always see it from the road. It was built in Winsted, Connecticut, some time before 1860 for a clock manufacturer's horses and wagons. It was dismantled and moved to its present site in recent years and is now a semi-private museum with a marvelous display of antique carriages, sleighs and other vehicles. When it was rebuilt, the present owners carefully added several elements that they had salvaged elsewhere. The Gothic bay windows, for example, came from an old church and parsonage that were torn down for a development. The beautiful horse stalls are made of materials from the lieutenant governor's old mansion in New Brunswick, Canada.

Above: A much simpler Connecticut carriage house that is connected to a barn—a rare arrangement.

Traveling down the Maine coast on U.S. Route 1, you cannot fail to exclaim over the homes built by wealthy 19th Century ship owners, sea captains and merchants. A great many of these have carriage houses; and in most cases, carriage house and residence are connected. This was undoubtedly done for the same reason that we build attached garages now. Here are two fine examples (although the trees screen the house in the picture opposite). Notice below how the same under-eaves brackets were used on both carriage house and residence.

The house built by W.H. Stark in Orange, Texas, in 1894 is a colossal Victorian, and even the carriage house (left) is of mansion size. The detailing (opposite page) is something to marvel at. Below is a much simpler Texas carriage house now used as a garage.

A Maine carriage house with a Mansard roof and balcony overhanging the carriage entrance.

At one time this Vermont carriage house may also have done duty as a farm barn. The dormered loft door is strangely positioned. It probably was centered over the carriage door, then slipped out of place, so to speak, when the door was widened for automobiles.

Left: Carriage house on the Maine coast. The arched loft door in the front gable softens the building's severe lines. Above: A very small brick carriage house on a Mississippi plantation. Built about 1832, it is, like the residence, in the Greek Revival style.

Today's home builders should take a lesson from the handsome house and its attached carriage house below: When you build a fine home, you should take pains to put up an equally fine garage.

The picture opposite carries the same lesson. This is a beautifully integrated design and plan. Both homes are in the same town on the Maine coast.

Opposite, top: Because this Maine carriage house was set below the residence, the two were connected by a raised, covered passageway built at the first-floor level of the residence. Opposite, bottom: Carriage house in a Boston suburb. The photo to the contrary, it is detached from the main house. Above: An enormous, ornate carriage house on a hill in an old Pennsylvania mining town. Now more or less abandoned, it is a monument to the past.

Another example of the way Maine builders integrated residence and carriage house in plan and treatment.

This Maine carriage house is massive, although not so massive as the house (unseen to the left). The hip roof is crowned by a small belvedere from which the owners, if so inclined, could look out to sea.

Above is a Connecticut carriage house of classic lines and proportions. The garage doors spoil the picture but could not be helped. Opposite, top: This Mississippi carriage house suggests a Greek temple. It distracts attention from the bigger but simpler barn. Bottom: Carriage house serving a church parsonage in Pennsylvania. It's an odd mixture of simplicity and ornamentation.

Old stable on the world's most famous farm—the King Ranch at Kingsville, Texas.

STABLES

More stables on the King Ranch, which is famed not only for its hundreds of thousands of acres and Santa Gertrudis cattle but also for its quarter horses and thoroughbreds. All the buildings are built of brick as a safeguard against disastrous fire. The pictures at bottom are of the same stable, front and back. It would take a mighty effort by a horse to kick out his heavy stall door.

The small barns in Parker, Texas (see text) are simple, neat, attractive. Each is a little different. Few are prefabs but many are built of plywood, flakeboard or similar siding materials.

Another Parker, Texas, stable seen from front and back. The owner also keeps a few sheep.

182

This three-horse Mississippi stable was built by the owner. Allowed to weather naturally, it is rather rustic yet pleasant. Known as a pole barn, it is supported by preservative-treated poles (dark timber in right photo) set into the ground on concrete footings. The top-plates are bolted to them. Usually two plates are used, one on the outside and the other on the inside of the poles.

Because he liked the extra hay and feed storage space gained in the forebays of Pennsylvania Dutch barns, the builder of the Connecticut stable at right projected the second story over the first and provided a recessed open area outside several of the stalls.

184

Left and below: One of Lexington, Kentucky's magnificent horse barns. Others are even larger and more beautiful, but you can't visit them without special permission. The present owner of this barn cannot explain why it has a belvedere unless it was formerly used for surveying the horses in the surrounding fields.

A relatively small Kentucky stable between Lexington and Louisville. The unique gambrel-roofed dormers containing the hay-loft doors match not only the roof of the entrance porch but also those on the entire building. The brick panels under the stall windows are a pleasant contrast to the vertical board siding.

Prefabricated metal barns are widely advertised to and widely used by horse owners. They come in many sizes but all are essentially like this one in Tennessee. Simple wood trusses support the metal roof.

A Connecticut stable with an indoor riding ring. The stalls surround the square ring, which is well lighted by numerous big skylights, on all four sides. They have wood and heavy wire-mesh sides and wire-mesh inside doors so the horses can see one another. Horses are very social animals and like companionship.

This Connecticut stable measures 180 x 110 feet. The stalls run down one side (under the lowest part of the roof) and the remaining space is taken up by a 180 x 80 foot riding ring lighted by big strip windows on three sides. The roof over the ring is supported on enormous steel trusses and trussed wood rafters.

The Magnificent New Private Stable of Adolphus Busch. Esq.

An Equine Palace — All Horse lovers should visit.

NOTWITHSTANDING the extraordinarily busy life led by Adolphus Busch, who is the mainspring in the vast machine which has worked such wonders, he finds time to cultivate an ardent love for the horse. He is not what would be called a sporting man, or fast stock fancier, because, while he has admiration for speed, his fondness is based rather upon the nobility, the intelligence, the patience, the amiability and the affectionate characteristics of the animal, than upon its mere powers of motion. The man who loves a horse—not merely fancies it—finds an easy road to Mr. Busch's good will, and men who devote themselves to the improvement of breeds, are regarded by him as public benefactors. The fine stock men of the country, therefore, may accept as a personal compliment the fact that the very handsomest architectural feature among all the costly buildings that cover the forty-seven blocks of brewery property, is the private stable of Mr. Busch. It was made beautiful, not because of a desire for ostentation, because the very simple and democratic habits of Mr. Busch negative such an idea, but it was made such a conspicuous feature in the hope that it would carry a lesson to all who own horses, few or many. It has long been a pet theory with Mr. Busch that there was no good reason why an animal as cleanly, as orderly, and as free from destructive disposition as a horse, should not be housed as comfortably and with as much regard for sightliness as a human being. He believed it was not only the humane, but the economical view, for long experience with hundreds of horses has taught him that the well-kept and well-treated animal does better work and more of it than the horse which eats, and sleeps, and "rests" in coldness, dampness and darkness. He long ago put this theory into practice, and the hundreds of sleek, contented, powerful, good-natured horses which do the brewery work, are irrefutable evidence of the correctness of his views. In his private stables, he aimed to bring this idea to the notice of the public in such form as to fix their attention. To that end he gave the building a commanding site, constructed it of the finest stock brick, on an octagonal design, gave it liberal and tasty ornamentation, lighted it as he would a dwelling, and beautified the ground surrounding it. The interior, arranged something on the plan of a locomotive roundhouse, with all parts opening into a common centre, gives proof of the same care of decoration that would be ordinarily bestowed upon a costly dwelling. A superintendent's office, waiting room and billiard room are very attractive and tasty features of the interior, and the horses in their stalls are far more comfortable than many well-to-do people in their homes. The many ladies who visit the place find the trip to be a great pleasure, rather than an ordeal.

The building, which cost $35,000, has dimensions 95x110 feet. The walls of the entrance passage, wash room, stable proper, and carriage room are faced on the inside with selected stock brick and enameled brick wainscoting and band courses; the base in these rooms is of polished stone, while all exposed corners of brick work are protected by ornamental iron guards. The stable proper is fitted up with paneled hard-wood; stall partitions surmounted by wrought-iron scroll stall guards; stall floors are of clay, with an underlayer of cinders, well packed; floors of waiting and hostler's rooms and billiard room are of hard-wood, and for all other rooms and passages, of Portland cement.

The waiting room is finished in quartered oak, with richly paneled wainscoting and mantel; remainder of building is finished in polished Florida pine. Harness closets are also of Florida pine, with glass-paneled doors. Plumbing is executed in the most complete manner, with nickel-plated faucets, Tennessee marble top wash basins, all English earthenware sinks, and the whole thoroughly trapped and ventilated. The entire building is heated by steam and lighted by electricity. Glazing in all the principal rooms is done with cathedral glass of variegated hues. The exterior is faced with round pitched range work and hydraulic-press brick, with colored joints and terra cotta trimmings.

The magazine story reproduced on Page 191 was published when the famous Busch stable in St. Louis was built in the 1880s, and tells the story more than adequately. All pictures are old. The stable still houses the Clydesdales used in Anheuser-Busch advertising and is open to the public.

192

The rice-growing country in Arkansas abounds with barns like this. Many are less graceful and many are larger, but all have a big rectangular top growing out of the roof. They are rice-drying and storage barns and were widely built after World War II when farmers began to dry the grain artificially rather than in the fields. But on many farms they have been succeeded by a newer type of drying barn of less interest.

Midwestern corn cribs are rather similar to the old rice barns in that they, too, have "top-knots", but they are smaller and of simpler design. In the cribs, unshelled corn is sluiced into the top-knots from outside until the cribs are loaded right up to the main roof ridge. But rice barns are used differently. The threshed grain is piled into the center of the barn, and on warm, dry days a large fan blows air into and through it. The air then exits up the chimney—that's all the top-knot really is—and escapes to the outdoors through openings in the sides.

SPECIAL-PURPOSE BARNS

A big hog farm like this one in Ohio has a collection of barns. The large red barn houses farm machinery and feed. Behind it is a huge shed for young hogs. The other red barn is used for maidens to be bred. A smaller building is occupied by the boars. And there are numerous little A-frame farrowing houses for summer use. On this farm, all the old buildings once served other purposes. The building at right is new. It's a farrowing house and connected behind it is a matching nursery. Both are prefabs made and fitted out specifically for the purpose. They were dropped off a trailer onto their foundations just as you see them here.

There are chicken houses and chicken houses. The large ones are enormous, long, one to three-story buildings that look like factories. Small ones can be anything at all. This neat red one in Pennsylvania is of medium size, a traditional design. It faces south for warmth; has clerestory windows to bring in extra warmth and light as well as to improve ventilation. The smaller building at the right is a duck house.

Below is a goat barn in Texas. The long wings were added to the original structure as the herd was expanded. At right is a tiny Mississippi barn that cannot house many more animals than the family pictured. Because of the warm climate, the windows are not glazed; but wire mesh keeps the goats from leaping through the openings. And the door is heavily braced to prevent destruction by a fractious beast.

Above: A small sheep barn in Iowa. Right: One of the big sheep barns at the Ohio Agricultural Research and Development Center in Wooster, Ohio. Except for the fact that each animal does not have a stall, sheep barns are not very different from cow barns. The Ohio barn is connected to a large conventional barn that is also used for sheep.

The central building in each of these pictures is not called a barn but is big enough to be one. These are midwestern corn cribs, the red one in Iowa, the white one in Wisconsin. The small structures atop the roofs are used for loading in unshelled corn. Because of them, the cribs can be filled to the very top. At the left of the white crib is a hog shed.

Tobacco barns are among the most interesting barns. They are almost invariably very long, narrow, tall buildings. Connecticut River tobacco growers figure they need one 100 x 30-foot barn to dry three acres of tobacco leaf. Good ventilation is as important as size. To achieve this in Pennsylvania long wall panels are pivoted to swing open (opposite, top). In Kentucky, the panels are hinged to open like doors (above, left). In Connecticut, the panels (really single wide boards) are nailed at the top and bent open and propped at the bottom (directly above). To facilitate this operation, four or five alternate boards are nailed to 2 x 4s so all can be opened together. The amount of air this lets in is shown in the interior photo. Further to enhance ventilation, most barns have lots of roof ventilators or have big openings like hay-loft doors in the gables. In the Kentucky barn at left a long strip ventilator is used. Incidentally, the latter barn is black. About half of the Kentucky tobacco barns and some of the horse barns are painted this unusual color.

202

Cupolas on barns and carriage houses bear little resemblance to the stock cupolas available today. They are bigger, and more varied—and a great deal prettier, as the pictures here and on the next four pages show. The barns on the facing page are in Illinois (top, left), Maine (top, right) and Vermont (bottom). The one above is in Iowa, where cupolas are less common than metal ventilators. Most Iowa cupolas are like this one.

FUNCTIONAL AND DECORATIVE FEATURES

Maine

Connecticut

New Jersey

New Jersey

New Hampshire

Maine

Mississippi

Ohio

Mississippi

Since we live in an age when cupolas are used mainly for decoration, it must be remembered that on barns they were meant for ventilation. Accordingly, most had louvered side openings as on the New Jersey barn opposite, top, and the Connecticut barn above. If they had glass, as on the New Jersey barn opposite, bottom, someone had to climb up inside the cupola to open and close it. On the barn above, note the extensive ornamentation of the gable and the gingerbread at the gable peak of the cupola. The cupola at left is an antique copper ventilator. It is one of a pair rescued from a decrepit Vermont barn and now gracing a house.

Opposite: The ventilating holes made in barn walls were sometimes slits, but the Pennsylvania Dutchmen favored more decorative designs even in thick masonry. In the New York Dutch barn of wood, the small holes are like inverted cocktail glasses.

Above: In old barns the hay-loft opening was right under the roof peak. In new barns such as this one in Iowa, it is generally lower so that the elevator used to hoist hay bales can be extended well back into the barn. The opening is also smaller, as a rule.

Opposite: In sunny California there is little need for a rain-hood over the hay-loft door. In this old barn the hayfork hangs from a track suspended from the ridge-pole and slides back into the barn. (Photo by Hal Simkover.) Rain-hoods are widely used in other parts of the country but vary in design. At right is a brand new architect-designed Connecticut barn with a unique hood. Below that is an old Connecticut barn. The hood on the Ohio barn directly below is so enveloping that a loft door is not needed. At bottom is an Illinois barn.

The louvered wall openings in the Pennsylvania Dutch barns around Sunbury are frequently very large and elaborate. Such openings are uncommon in other areas but do pop up on scattered barns here and there. The barn right, for instance, is in Ohio. On the grey slate roof in dark grey numerals is a date— 1882, the year in which the barn was constructed.

The owner of the Ohio bank barn at left decorated the big doors with hourglasses. Installation of the doors in the side of the rainbow roof necessitated the graceful ski-jump roof over the large bay containing the doors. Below: This large Ohio barn has arches painted on the doors. Here and there around the country are other barns with doors treated in this way. Right: Maine farmers go in rarely for fancy paint jobs, but the owner of this barn did. He even painted his two barns differently. This is very unusual everywhere.

Who in the world would think of painting portraits of Beethoven

and Rembrandt on the gable walls of barns? A Michigan farmer.

218

Miranda S. Burnett

Opposite, top: Artwork by a Pennsylvania peach grower. Bottom: This Ohio barn is called the Pine Tree Barn on a highway sign. It is the working and sales headquarters of a farm raising conifers. The pine trees on the white doors are windows.

Above: A barn and silo on Michigan's Leelanau Peninsula was painted to celebrate our bicentennial and pay homage to the history of the immediate area. It displays the flag, George Washington, dates, the area map, an Indian, a logger, a view of Lake Michigan, a Michigan forest.

In times past, barn walls often were used as highway billboards. National advertisers such as Mail Pouch Tobacco agreed to paint a barn completely in exchange for the privilege of putting an ad on the highway side. (The barn above is in Pennsylvania.) Whether local firms such as the insurance business advertising on the Ohio barn opposite were as generous is doubtful, but there must have been some quid pro quo. The owner of the Michigan barn (left) just advertised himself.

On the facing page is an Ohio barn festooned with old farm implements and with a martin house on top. Barns with decorative trim are not so rare but not common either (this is less true of carriage houses and stables). Fancy touches are found mostly in Pennsylvania and New England. These examples are in Connecticut.

Closeup of the lovely trim on the small Connecticut bank
barn shown on Page 23. Most of the windows are arched.